Scottish Classical Guitar Collection Volume 1

Edited by James Akers

Copyright © 2019 GMI - Guitar & Music Institute

www.guitarandmusicinstitute.com

ISBN 978-1-9163024-1-9

First published in Great Britain in 2019 by GMI - Guitar & Music Institute

Cover painting - creative commons

TABLE OF CONTENTS

Sei Arie Nazionali Scozzesi: M. Giuliani

A WORD FROM THE AUTHOR

Scottish Romantic Guitar is a collection of intermediate and advanced pieces for classical guitar by leading composers of the 19th century, inspired by Scotland. While these pieces have previously been available from different sources, they are compiled here for the first time, in corrected editions, in one convenient volume.

Highlights include, Mauro Giuliani's beautiful settings of six favourite Scottish songs; Fernando Sor's masterful 'Variations on Ye Banks and Braes' and Johan Kaspar Mertz's dramatic evocation of the landscape of the Outer Hebrides, 'Fingal's Cave.'

This collection offers the guitarist a unique source of unfamiliar yet accessible repertoire that is both challenging and rewarding to play and which will appeal to any audience.

James Akers

Scottish Romantic Guitar

During the first half of the 19th century, a wave of interest in Scottish culture swept over Western Europe. The poetry of Ossian and Robert Burns, the epic historical novels of Sir Walter Scott and the wild unruly landscape itself provided inspiration for composers including Donizetti, Rossini and Mendelssohn.

While the publication of a book of traditional Scottish songs, *The Scot's Musical Museum,* in 1797 gave impetus for the exploration of the genre by such luminaries as Haydn and Beethoven. The classical guitar world, then going through its first historical 'golden age' was not immune to this influence and leading composers including Mauro Giuliani, Fernando Sor and Johann Kaspar Mertz were able to produce a small but unique repertoire of guitar music inspired by Scotland.

Fernando Sor's variations on the popular melody *Ye Banks and Braes*, opus 40, dates from around 1830 and was unknown before the 1970s, when it was discovered by the great guitar scholar Brian Jeffery. Only two copies survive of the original print.

Mauro Giuliani's *Sei Arie Nazionali Scozzesi* were published posthumously in 1834 and form a companion piece to his collection of Irish Airs, op.125. They contain settings of six Scottish tunes including such Hogmanay favourites as *Coming through the Rye* and *the Bluebells of Scotland.*

Though not based on a Scottish tune, Johann Kaspar Mertz's *Fingal's Cave* is included here as it takes its inspiration from the Scottish landscape, specifically a remote sea cave on the uninhabited island of Staffa, renowned for its acoustic properties. It comes from Mertz's vast compilation of his compositions, *Barden Klang* (Bardic sounds) and is unrelated to Mendlessohn's famous *Hebridean Overture.*

In 1825, the melody of *Robin Adair* featured prominently in the successful opera *La Dame Blanche* by Boieldieu. Subsequently, it became a popular vehicle for composers to employ in writing variations. Both Lhoyer and Molino rose to this challenge and produced substantial works based on the theme.

Editorial Method

The music in this volume has been transcribed from original sources. The only alterations that have been made are to correct obvious engraving errors. All performance directions and fingering instructions are from the original print and therefore, presumably, the composer's own work.

Variations on a Favourite Scottish Air

Variation 1

Variation 2
70
74
77
81
3 3 3 3
3 3 3 3
84
86
Variation 3
89
VII VII XII VII VII XII VII
4 2 1 3 3 2 4
6 3 6
93
VII XII VII XII VII
4 2 3 1 4
IX XII IX VII IX
6 3 6 4 5
7

The Soldier's Return

38
sf
p
Maggiore
41
mf
45
48
51
53
55
p
58
mf
60
f

This is no my ain lassie

Coming, Through the Rye

27
dolce
f
30
34
pp
36
pp
ff

Jenny's Bawbee, A Reel

M. Giuliani

127
p
f
mf
135
p
sf
sf
143
mf
150
sf > sf > f
mf
158
164
f
170
mf
f
178
183
f
sf

The Blue Bells of Scotland

The Old Country Bumpkin

pp

Fingal's Cave

19
21
23
25 dol.
27
29
31
cresc
tristamente
33
35
③ ③

37
39
41
43
44
cresc
45
46
48
cresc

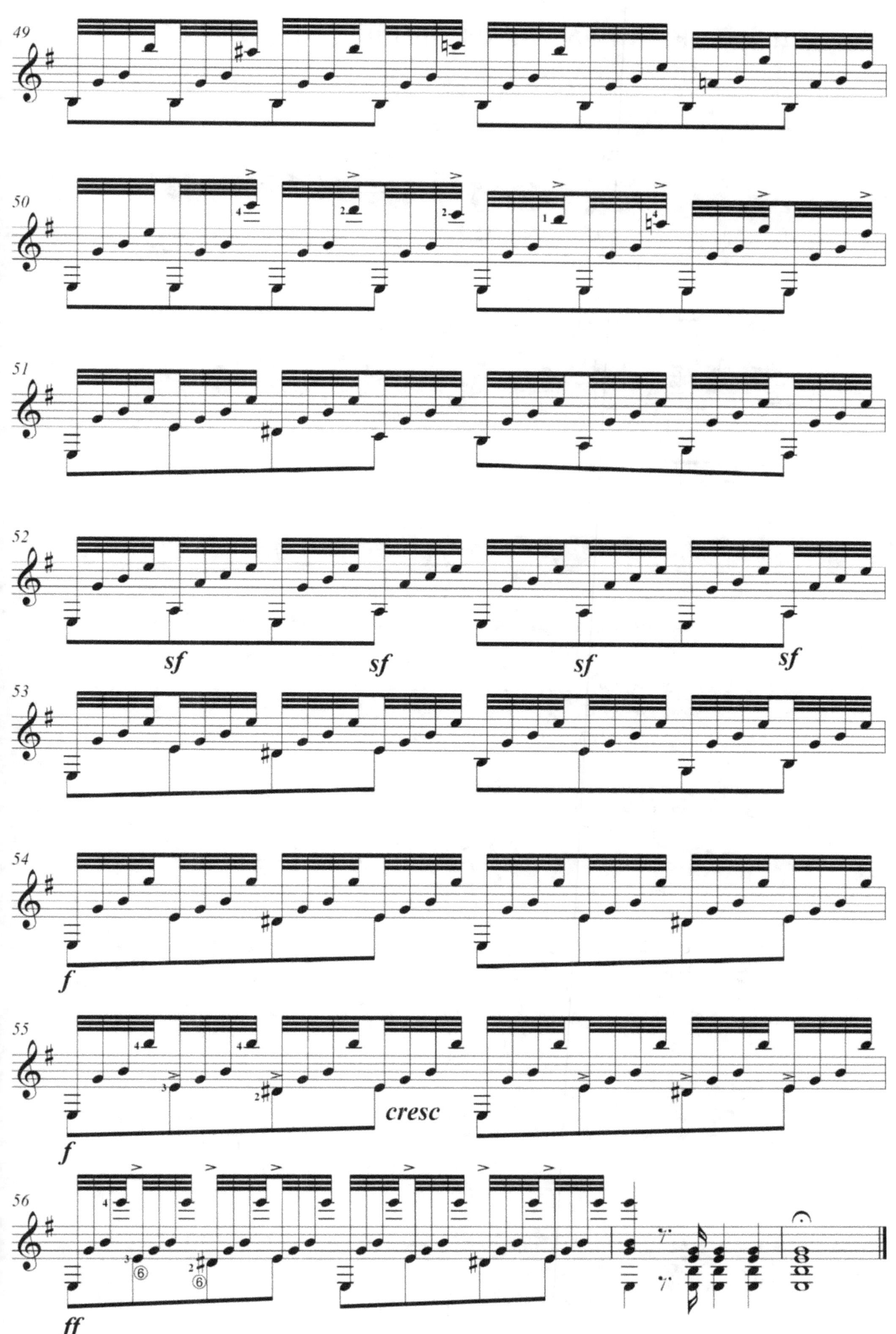

Introduction et Variations sur un Air Ecossais

Antoine de Lhoyer

38
42
46
Variation2
50
54
59
62
Variation 3
66
VII XII IX VII XII VII
VII XII IX VII XII VII
④ ② ⑤ ③ ① ②
④ ② ⑤ ③ ① ②

72
76
79
Variation 4
82
Minore, poco lento
p
88
sf
p
94
sf
p
98
100
6 6 6 6 6 6
ad libitum

Variation 5
tempo primo
102

105

108

112

116
poco lento

119
PP

Robin Adair

Introduction

F. Molino

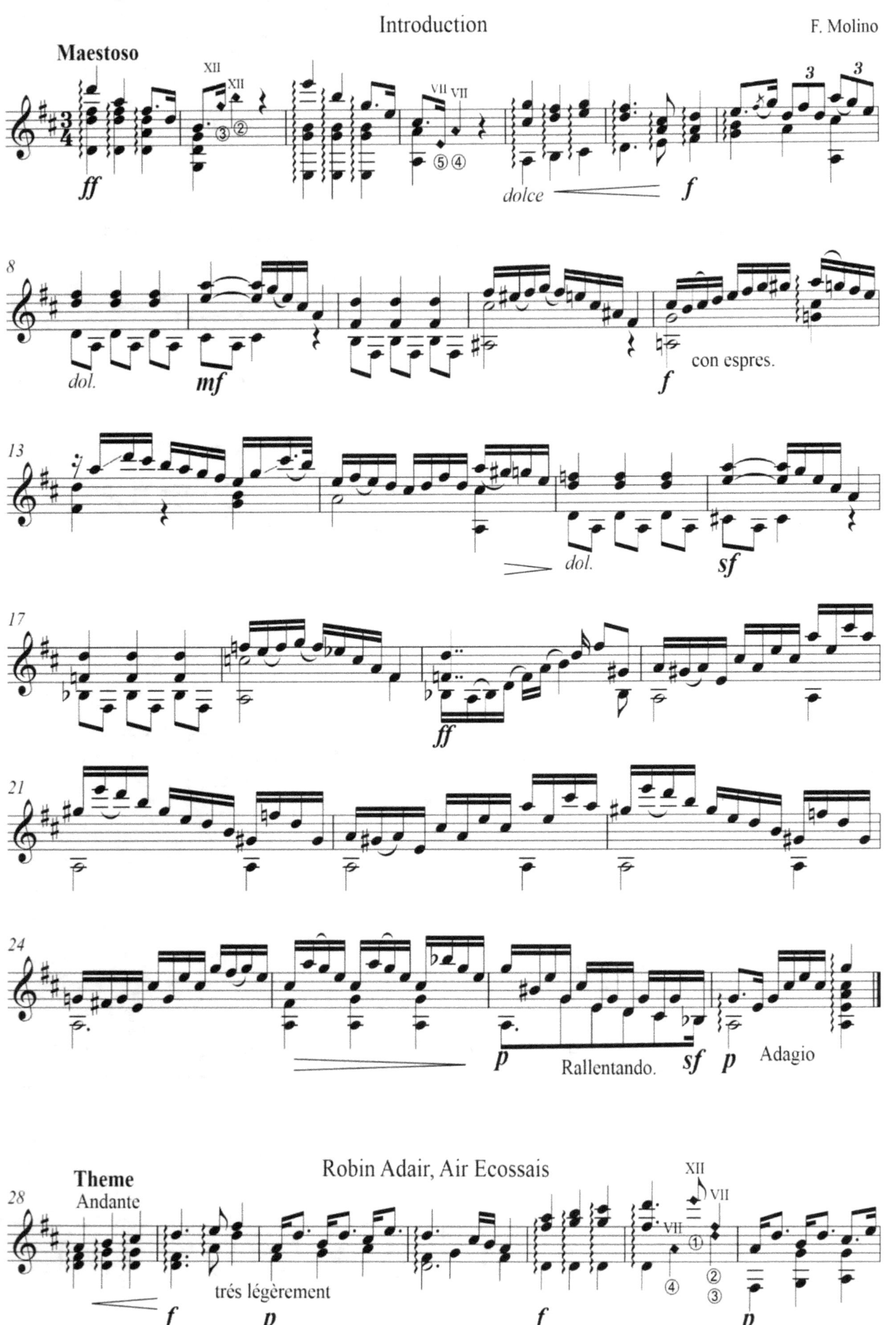

Variation 1
Variation 2
35
39
44
49
54
57
60
64
f
sf
dol.
con espres.
f
p
f
f
f
f
f
f

Variation 3
Variation 4
34

Explanation: *In this variation, the rests in the bars with the harmonics, which shouldn't be there, are solely intended to imitate the delay that always occurs when an echo reproduces a sound.**

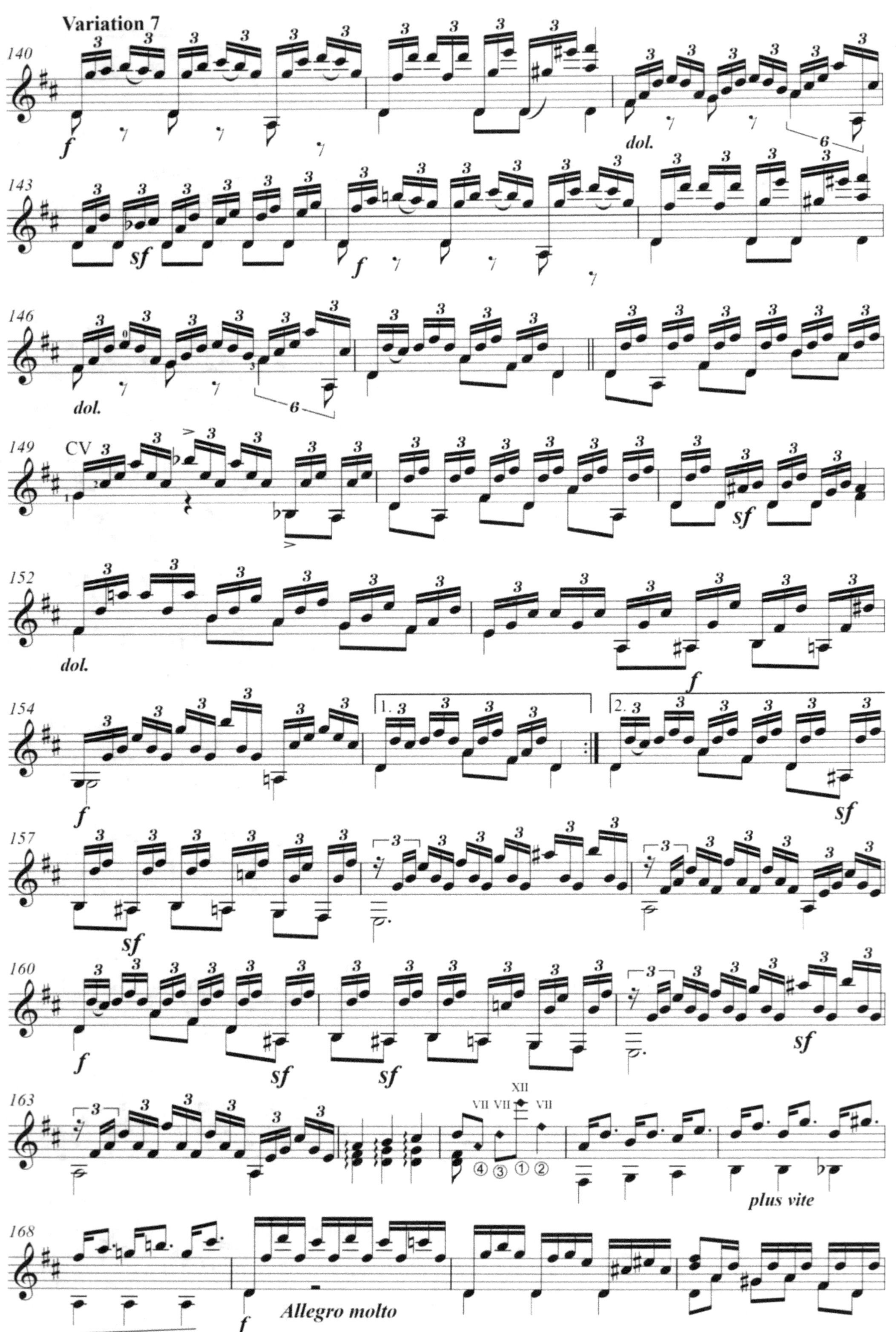

Variation 7
140
dol.
143
sf
f
146
dol.
149
CV
sf
152
dol.
154
1.
2.
f
f
sf
157
sf
160
f
sf
sf
sf
163
XII
VII VII VII
plus vite
168
Allegro molto
f

*the original instructions read, "*Dans cette Variation, le Soupir qui est place dans les measures où se trouvent les harmoniques, et qui ne devrait pas y entrer, est uniquement destine à imiter le retard que l'echo met toujours à reproduire les sons.*

About James Akers

Critically acclaimed musician Jamie Akers was hailed as 'the great Scottish guitarist' by Classical Guitar Magazine and, in a review from Gramophone, his playing was described as, 'containing all the warmth, colour and expressive richness one could hope for.' Jamie has, throughout a varied career, explored various genres of music from a historical and stylistic perspective, combining diligent research with expressive performances to communicate the continuity of musical endeavour through the centuries.

Jamie was born in Scotland and began playing guitar at the age of 10. Initially playing rock and blues then attempting to play jazz and finally settling on the classical guitar, he was largely self-taught before having lessons with Robert Mackillop at Napier University, Edinburgh. Whilst at Napier he turned his attentions to playing the lute and pursued this as his principle study at the Royal College of Music, with Jakob Lindberg. Having added the Theorbo to his expanding instrument collection, Jamie completed his studies at Trinity College of Music, studying with Jacob Heringman and David Miller, with additional lessons and advice from Paul O'Dette and Elizabeth Kenny. Settled on the period instrument path, Jamie continued accumulating instruments and exploring the music of the 16th to 19th centuries, with occasional forays into contemporary music.

Following a Junior Fellowship at Trinity College of Music Jamie began pursuing a varied professional career. As a soloist he has performed throughout Europe, the Middle East and Australia, giving recitals at the Edinburgh Fringe Festival, Ullapool Guitar Festival, Classical Guitar Retreat, Exeter Guitar Festival, the Yorke Music Trust, the Italian Cultural Institute, in the L'Oratoire de Lourve, and the Copenhagen Renaissance Music Festival.

He has accompanied leading singers including Dame Emma Kirkby, James Laing, Miriam Allan, Claire Wilkinson and Jake Arditti and is the staff accompanist for the John Kerr memorial song prize. Jamie has performed with many early music ensembles such as I Fagiolini, Ex Cathedra, Stile Antico, the Marian Consort, Fretwork, Chelys Viol Consort, The Rose Consort of Viols, The Parley of Instruments, The Hanover Band, The Brook Street Band, Sounds Baroque and the Dunedin Consort.

As a continuo player Jamie has worked for major opera companies, English National Opera, Welsh National Opera, Opera North, Longborough festival opera and Innsbruck Festival Opera and orchestras and chamber groups including The Scottish, Irish and English Chamber Orchestras, Northern Sinfonia, the Royal Scottish National Orchestra, The Ulster Orchestra, The Essen Philharmonie, The Scottish Ensemble, with trumpeter Alison Balsom, and ventured into indie folk-rock with Damon Albarn.

Jamie has performed on numerous recordings; a few film soundtracks; several theatrical stages, including Shakespeare's Globe Theatre and the Barbican, and broadcast for the BBC, France Musique and RTE Lyric, Ireland, and has been an artist in residence with the renowned Scottish Ensemble.

Jamie lectures in early plucked strings at the Royal Conservatoire of Scotland and teaches annually on the Renaissance Music Week course in Ejstrupholm, Denmark. He has also taught or given masterclasses at, The Royal College of Music, The Royal Northern College of Music, The Royal Welsh College of Music and Drama, the Western Australian Academy of Performing Arts and The Rostov Conservatoire, Russia.

http://jamieakers.com/

More From James Akers From GMI - Guitar & Music Institute

If you have enjoyed this book then we're sure you will also find James's transcriptions of Theorbo music for classical guitar a must buy.

Not only does the book include beautiful works by Kapsberger, Piccinini and Castaldi but this large publication also includes the following:

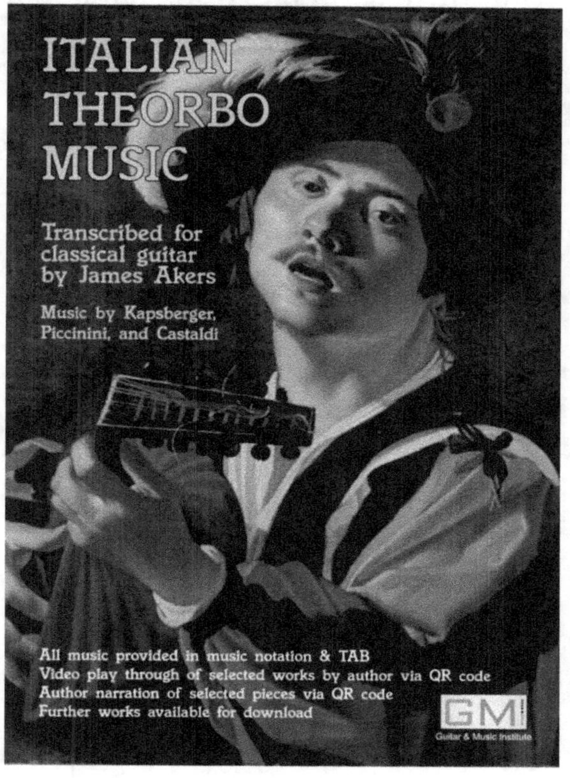

All works offered in both music and guitar tabulature.

Selected works include an audio commentary that is accessed via QR codes placed alongside specific titles. Use your mobile (cell) phone or tablet to listen to James's commentary from both a technical and musical perspective about the work you will be learning.

Selected works include a QR code that opens up a performance video of the piece currently being considered. Listen to this stellar guitarist play and interpret the musical composition for your guidance as well as listening pleasure.

Owners of the book will be able to access further musical works that accompany this publication. Your copy of this book will include a code which enables you to access this PDF download completely free of charge.

Italian Theorbo Music is available to purchase from Amazon and all other good online sellers in both printed and electronic format. A wire bound flat lie version of the book is available only from https://gmiguitarshop.com

An introduction PDF book containing extra works for pre sale of this book or as mentioned free for those who have already purchased the printed version is available to buy direct from the GMI - Guitar & Music Institute online shop at https://gmiguitarshop.com

RECORDING

James Akers' critically acclaimed recording of Scottish Romantic Guitar Music, The Soldier's Return, is available on CD and through various digital platforms.

Visit www.resonusclassics.com for more information.

If you enjoyed this publication, then please visit the following websites for more content, lessons, articles, videos, podcasts, free and paid content and more…

www.guitarandmusicinstitute.com

gmiguitarshop.com